Selections from
The WIZARD OF OZ
for Recorder

Easy Recorder Songbook

CONTENTS

Alfred Music Publishing Co., Inc.
16320 Roscoe Blvd., Suite 100
P.O. Box 10003
Van Nuys, CA 91410-0003
alfred.com

Book & Recorder
ISBN-10: 0-7390-5731-6
ISBN-13: 978-0-7390-5731-5

Book
ISBN-10: 0-7390-6064-3
ISBN-13: 978-0-7390-6064-3

About the Recorder

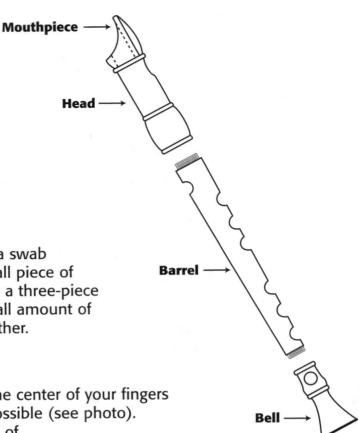

Parts of the Recorder

Although some recorders are made of one single piece, many are made up of three pieces that fit snugly together. The top is called the *head;* the middle is called the *barrel,* and the bottom is called the *bell.* The very top of the head is called the *mouthpiece,* which is the part of the recorder into which you blow.

Care of the Recorder

Each time you finish playing, it is important to run a swab through the recorder to dry all the moisture. A small piece of towel attached to a stick will work well. If you have a three-piece recorder, you may need to occasionally apply a small amount of cork grease to keep the sections from sticking together.

Holding the Recorder

When holding the recorder, it is important to use the center of your fingers to cover each hole, keeping the fingers as flat as possible (see photo). It is not correct to cover the holes with just the tips of the fingers.

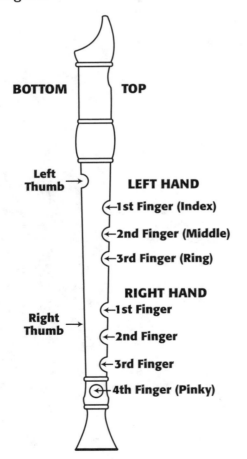

Playing the Recorder

Be sure not to put any more than one-half inch of the mouthpiece into your mouth. Touch the mouthpiece only with your lips, and be sure not to bite the mouthpiece with your teeth. When blowing into the instrument, it is important not to blow too hard. At first, play softly, because this will help you develop control. To begin a note, lightly tap your tongue against the roof of your mouth as if you were saying "tu."

Getting Acquainted with Music

Notes

Notes are used to indicate musical sounds. Some notes are long and others are short.

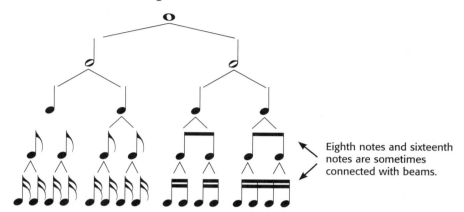

whole note   o   gets 4 beats

half note   gets 2 beats

quarter note   gets 1 beat

eighth note   gets ½ beat

sixteenth note   gets ¼ beat

Eighth notes and sixteenth notes are sometimes connected with beams.

When a *dot* follows a note, the length of the note is longer by one half of the note's original length.

dotted half note   gets 3 beats

dotted quarter note   gets 1½ beats

dotted eighth note   gets ¾ beat

Rests

Rests are used to indicate musical silence.

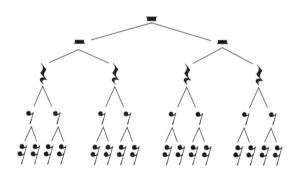

whole rest   gets 4 beats

half rest   gets 2 beats

quarter rest   gets 1 beat

eighth rest   gets ½ beat

sixteenth rest   gets ¼ beat

Staff

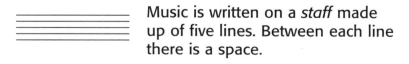

Music is written on a *staff* made up of five lines. Between each line there is a space.

line 5 ⟶ _____
line 4 ⟶ _____ ⟵ space 4
line 3 ⟶ _____ ⟵ space 3
line 2 ⟶ _____ ⟵ space 2
line 1 ⟶ _____ ⟵ space 1

In this book, you will see letters above the staff called *chord symbols* that can be played by a friend on another instrument such as a guitar or keyboard.

Treble Clef

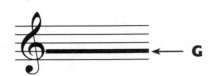

A *clef* is at the beginning of each line of music. The *treble clef*, also called the *G clef*, shows that the second line is the note G.

Notes on the Staff

E F G A B C D E F

Notes are named using the first seven letters of the alphabet (A B C D E F G).

The notes on the lines are:

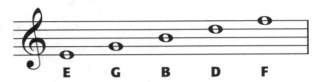

E G B D F

An easy way to remember this is the phrase "**E**very **G**ood **B**oy **D**oes **F**ine."

The notes in the spaces are:

F A C E

The way to remember this is the word **FACE**.

The staff can be extended to include even higher or lower notes by using *ledger lines*. This book uses the notes C and D below the bottom line of the staff.

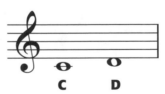

C D

In this book, every note has the note name inside of it to make playing the songs easier.

Measure
Music is divided into equal parts called *measures*.

Bar Lines
A *bar line* indicates where one measure ends and another begins.

Double Bar
A *double bar line*, made of one thin line and one thick line, shows the end of a piece of music.

Accidentals

An *accidental* raises or lowers the sound of a note. A *sharp* ♯ raises a note one half step. A *flat* ♭ lowers a note one half step. A *natural* ♮ cancels a sharp or flat. An accidental affects that note for the rest of that measure.

Fermata

A *fermata* 𝄐 over a note means to hold it about twice as long as usual.

Ties

A *tie* is a curved line that joins two or more notes of the same pitch. Instead of playing the second note, continue to hold for the combined note value.

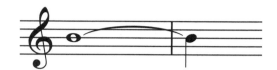

Hold for 5 beats.

Time Signature

4 = 4 beats to a measure

4 = quarter note ♩ gets 1 beat

6 = 6 beats to a measure

8 = eighth note ♪ gets 1 beat

Repeat Signs

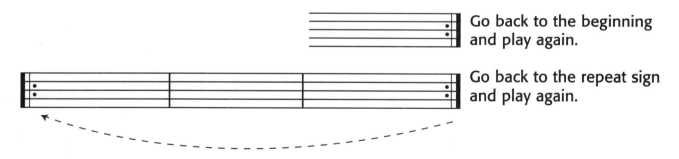

Go back to the beginning and play again.

Go back to the repeat sign and play again.

1st & 2nd Endings

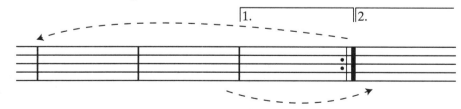

Play the 1st ending the first time, repeat, then skip the 1st ending and play the 2nd ending.

D.C. al Coda

Go back to the beginning and play to the coda sign (⊕), then skip to the coda to end the piece.

Let's Start Playing

Here are the notes you need to play Beethoven's "Ode to Joy." All of these notes are played with your left hand.

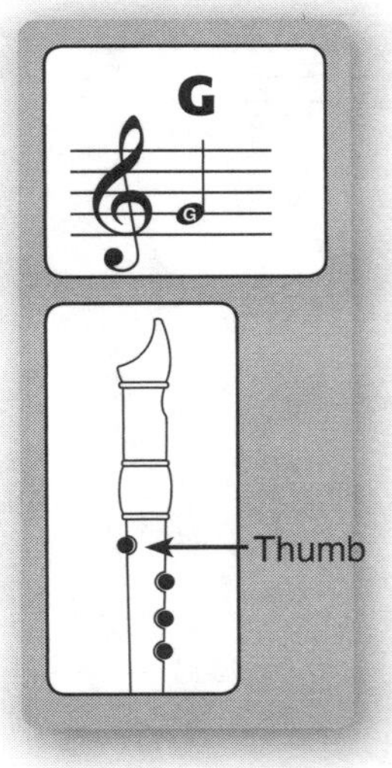

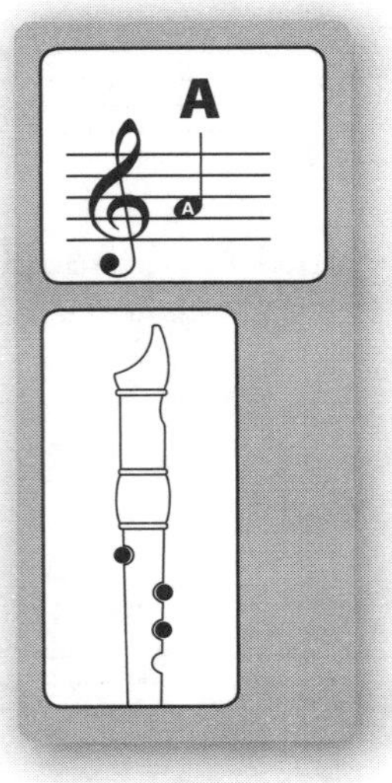

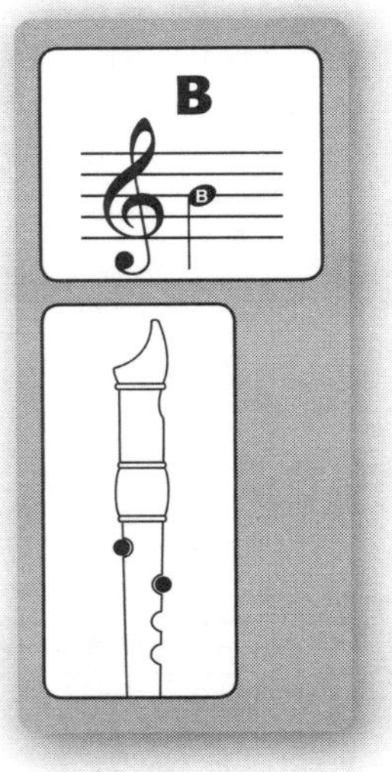

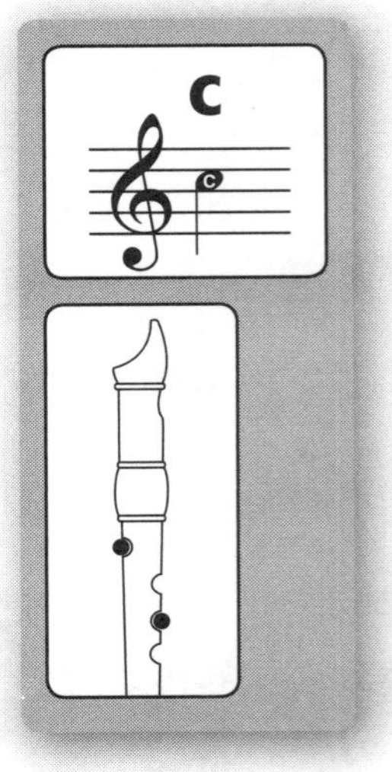

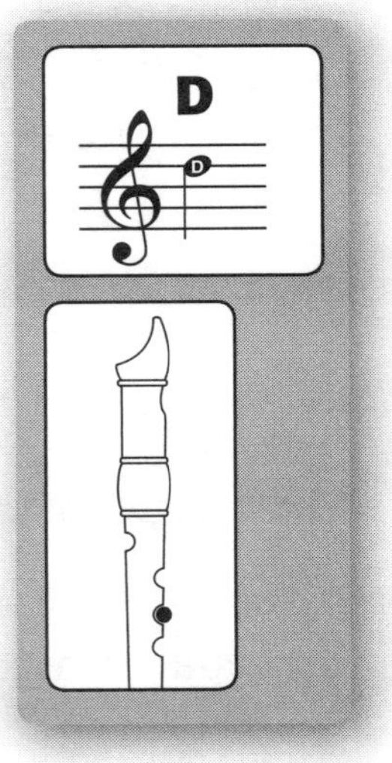

Remember: a quarter note ♩ gets 1 beat, and a half note 𝅗𝅥 gets 2 beats. Keep the beats even.

Ode to Joy

Ludwig van Beethoven

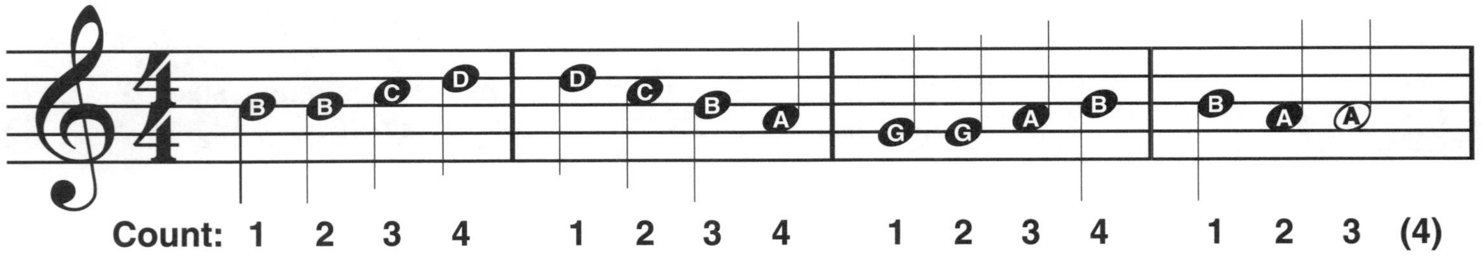

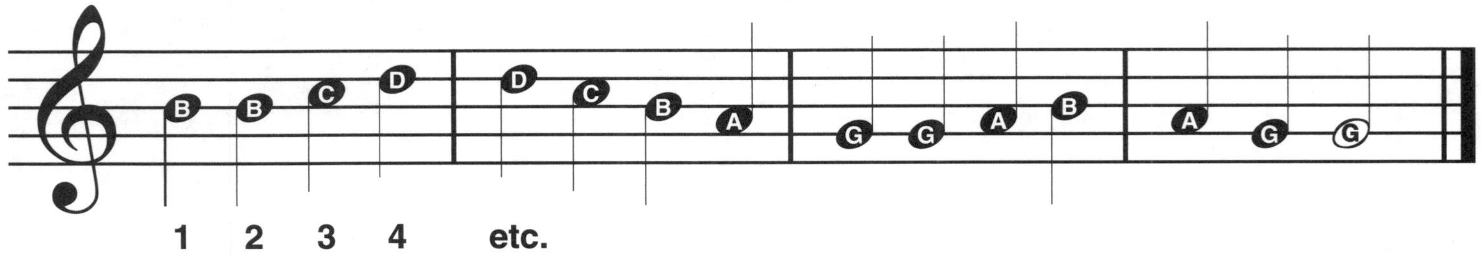

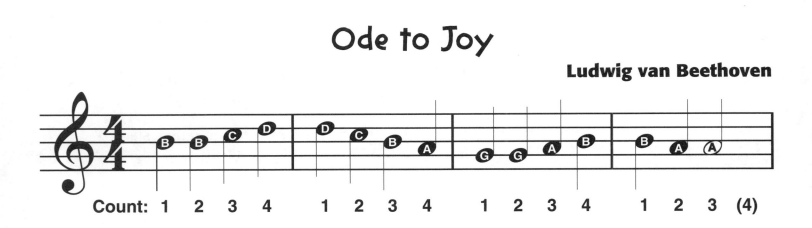

Adding Your Right Hand

For "Alouette," you will use your right hand to finger the note D.

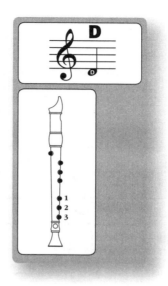

Remember: a whole note ○ gets 4 beats, and a quarter rest ⸰ gets 1 beat of silence.

Alouette

French folk song

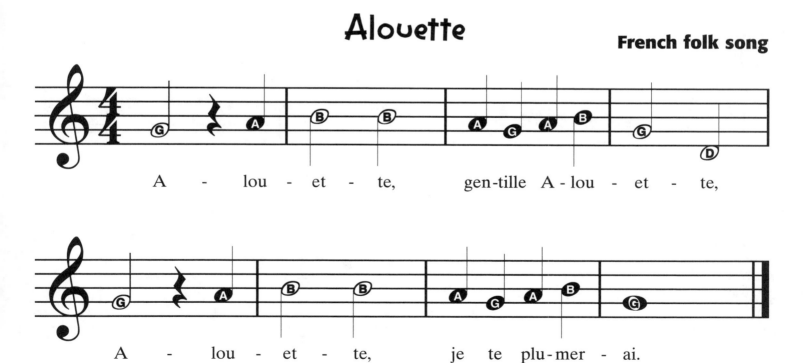

Complete Fingering Chart

● Closed Hole

◡ Partially Closed Hole

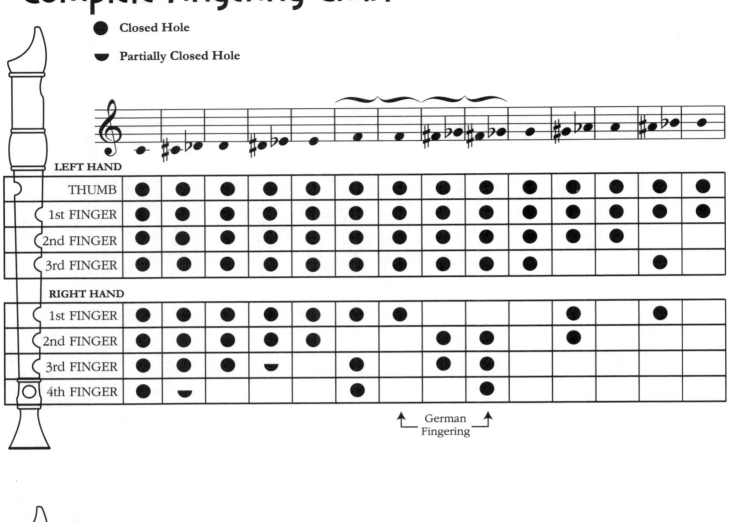

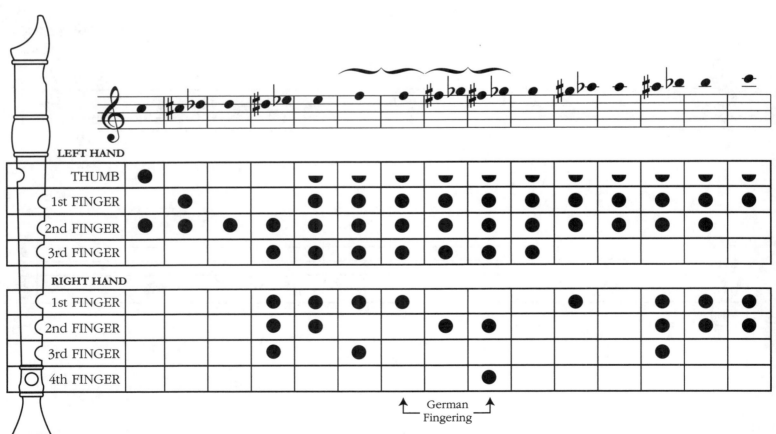

DING-DONG! THE WITCH IS DEAD

Lyrics by
E. Y. HARBURG

Music by
HAROLD ARLEN

Moderately bright

Ding - dong, the witch is dead!
Wake up, you witch sleep - y head.

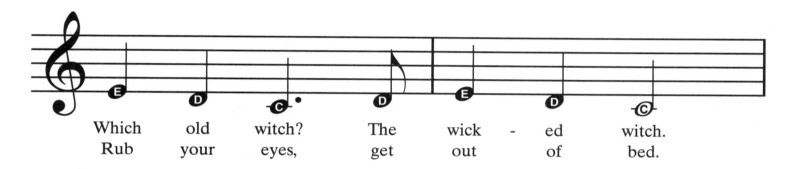

Which old witch? The wick - ed witch.
Rub your eyes, get out of bed.

1.

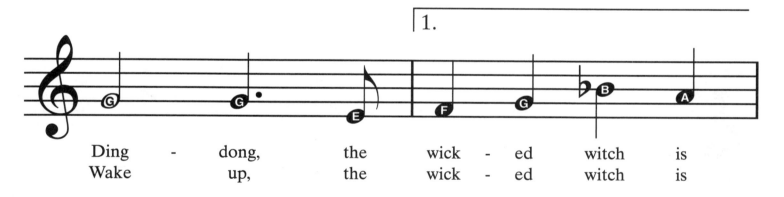

Ding - dong, the wick - ed witch is
Wake up, the wick - ed witch is

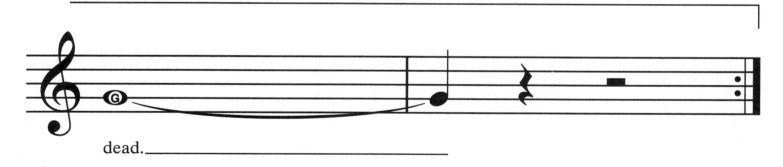

dead._____

Ding-Dong! The Witch Is Dead - 3 - 1
31909

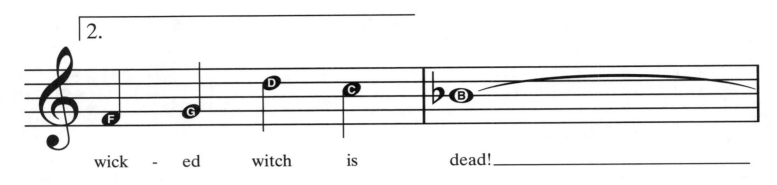

wick - ed   witch   is   dead!

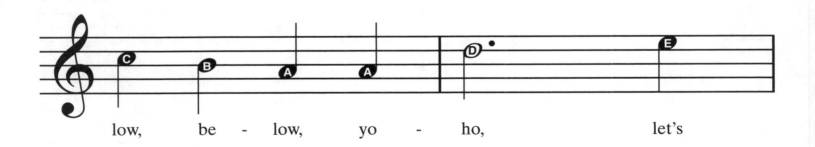

_____   She's   gone   where   the

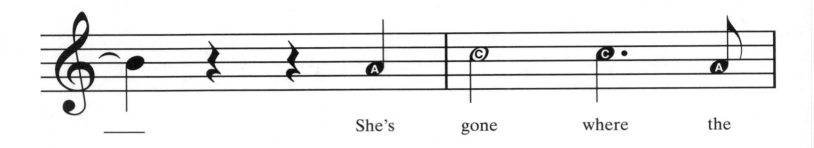

gob - lins   go   be - low,   be -

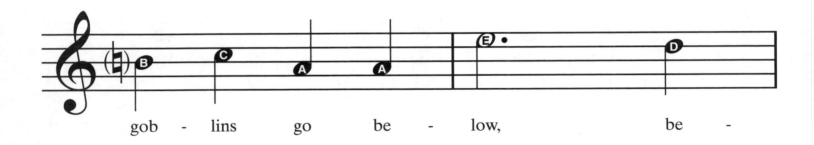

low,   be - low,   yo - ho,   let's

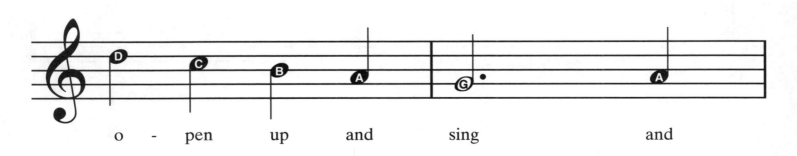

o - pen   up   and   sing   and

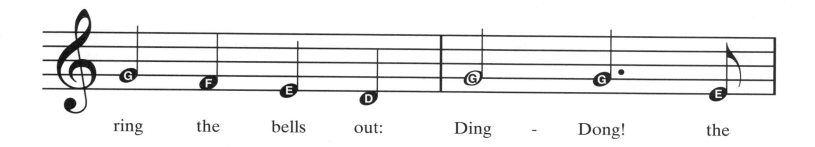

ring   the   bells   out: Ding - Dong!   the

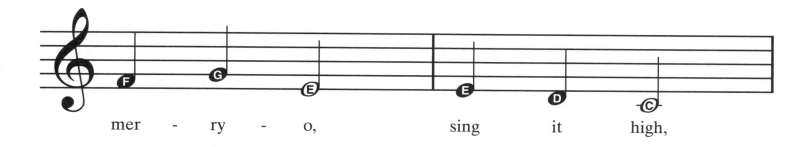

mer - ry - o,   sing   it   high,

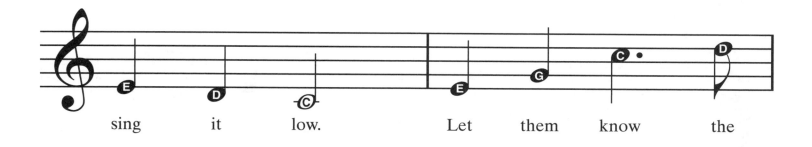

sing   it   low.   Let   them   know   the

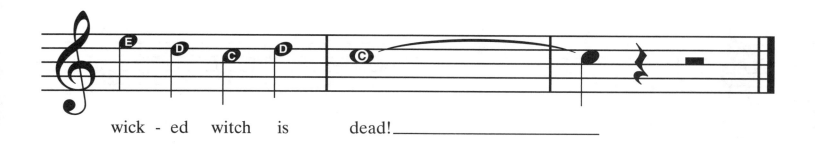

wick - ed   witch   is   dead!_____

Ding-Dong! The Witch Is Dead - 3 - 3
31909

IF I ONLY HAD A BRAIN

Lyrics by
E. Y. HARBURG

Music by
HAROLD ARLEN

Moderate swing

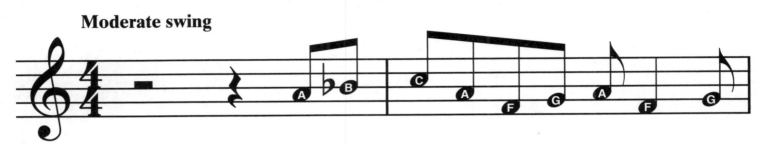

I could while a - way the hours___ con -

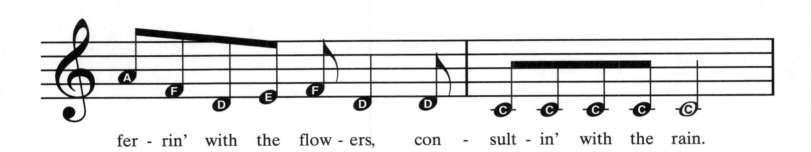

fer - rin' with the flow - ers, con - sult - in' with the rain.

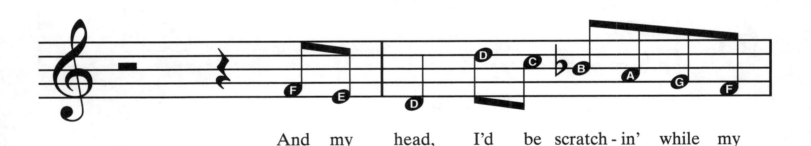

And my head, I'd be scratch - in' while my

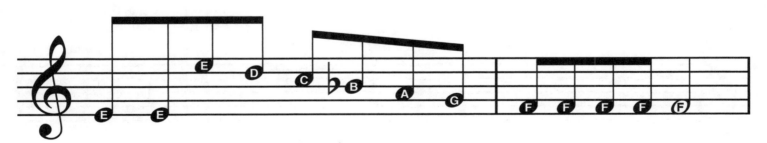

thoughts were bus - y hatch - in' if I on - ly had a brain.

If I Only Had a Brain - 3 - 1
31909

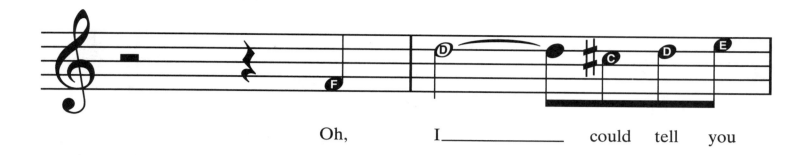

Oh,   I_____ could tell you

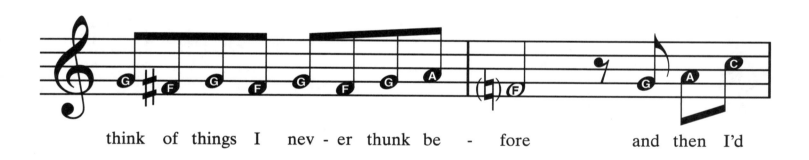

why   the   o - cean's near the   shore,   I could

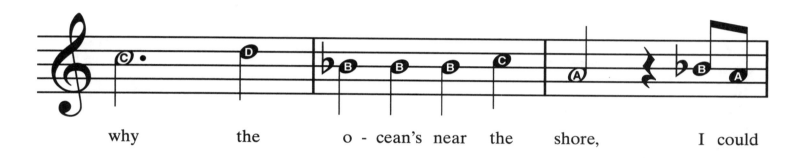

think of things I nev - er thunk be - fore   and then I'd

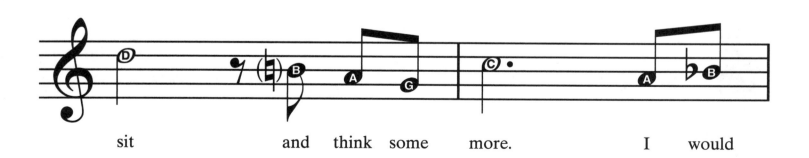

sit   and think some   more.   I   would

not be just a nuff‑in', my head all full of stuff‑in', my

heart all full of pain. And per ‑

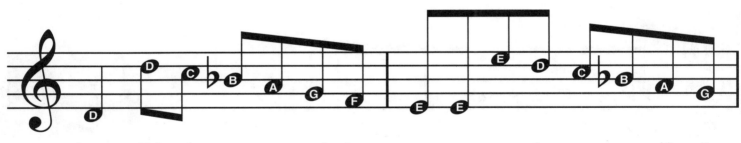

haps I'd de‑serve you and be e‑ven wor‑thy erv you if I

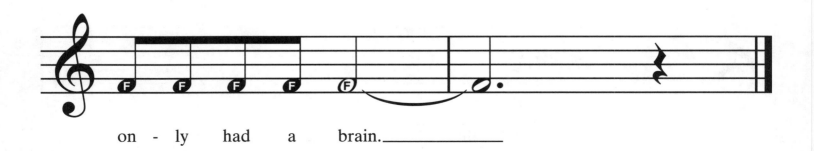

on‑ly had a brain._____

THE MERRY OLD LAND OF OZ

Lyrics by
E. Y. HARBURG

Music by
HAROLD ARLEN

Moderately, with spirit

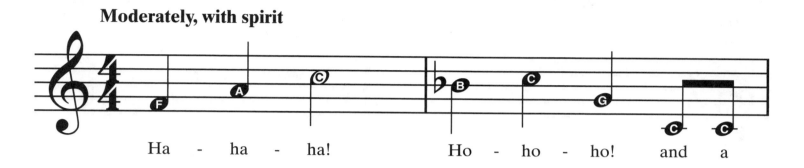

Ha - ha - ha!   Ho - ho - ho!   and a

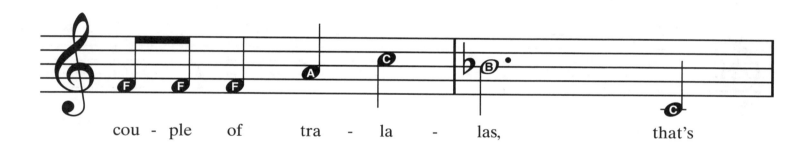

cou - ple of tra - la - las,   that's

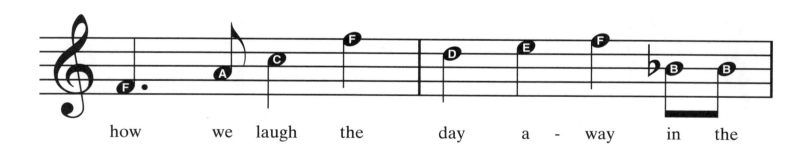

how we laugh the day a - way in the

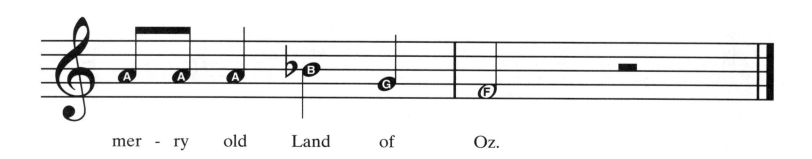

mer - ry old Land of Oz.

LULLABY LEAGUE AND LOLLIPOP GUILD

Lyrics by
E. Y. HARBURG

Music by
HAROLD ARLEN

Moderately fast

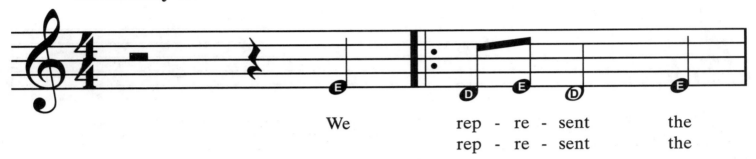

We rep - re - sent the
rep - re - sent the

Lul - la - by League, the Lul - la - by League, the
Lol - li - pop Guild, the Lol - li - pop Guild, the

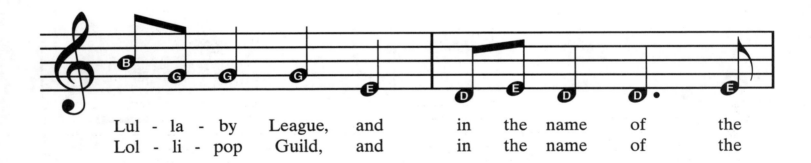

Lul - la - by League, and in the name of the
Lol - li - pop Guild, and in the name of the

Lul - la - by League, we wish to wel - come you to
Lol - li - pop Guild, we wish to wel - come you to

Lullaby League and Lollipop Guild - 2 - 1
31909

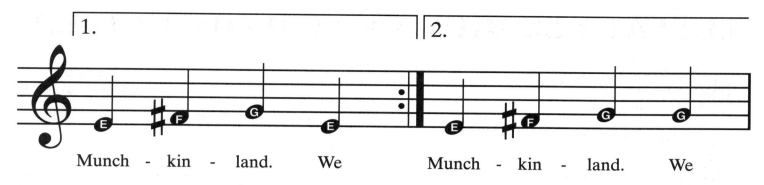

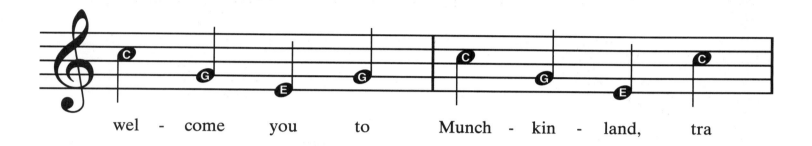

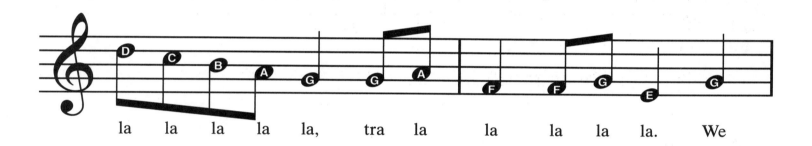

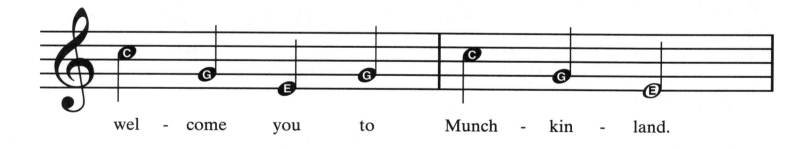

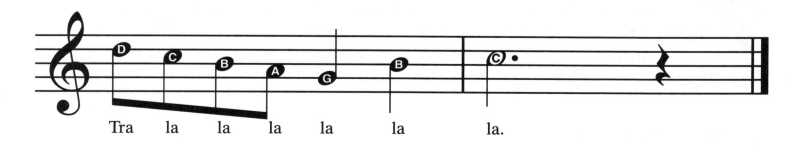

OPTIMISTIC VOICES

Lyrics by
E. Y. HARBURG

Music by
HAROLD ARLEN

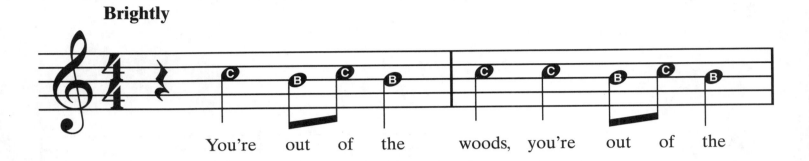

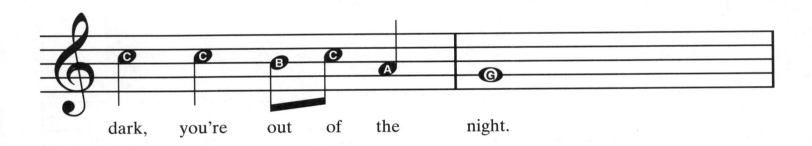

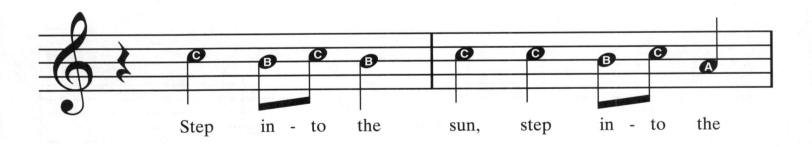

Optimistic Voices - 3 - 1
31909

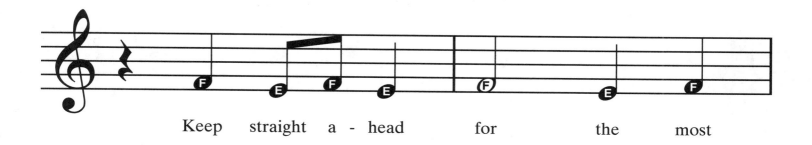

Keep straight a - head for the most

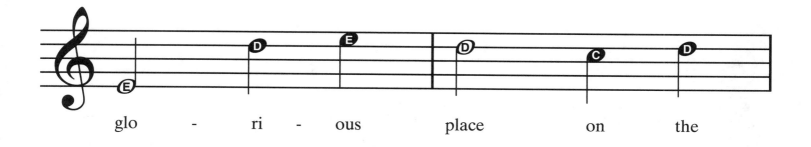

glo - ri - ous place on the

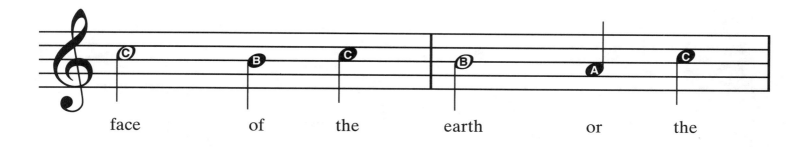

face of the earth or the

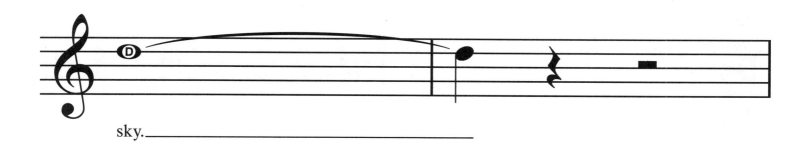

sky._____

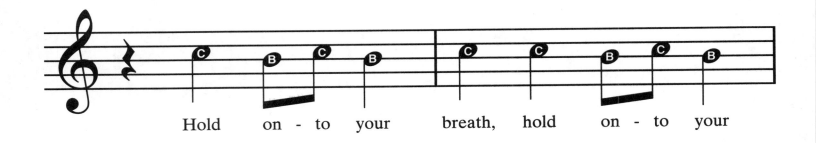

Hold on - to your breath, hold on - to your

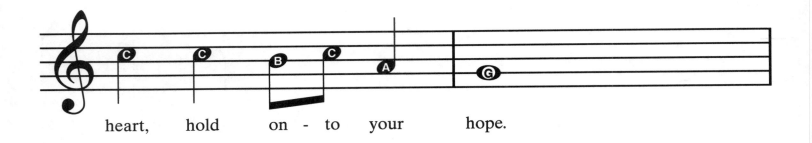

heart, hold on - to your hope.

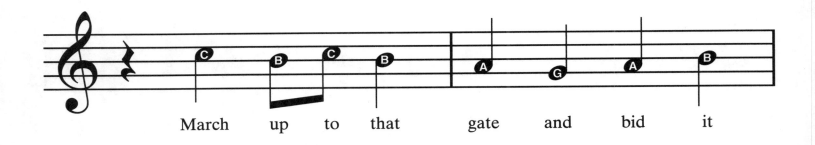

March up to that gate and bid it

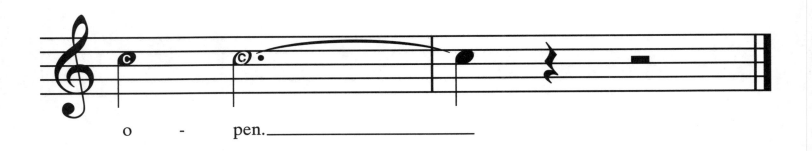

o - pen.

WE'RE OFF TO SEE THE WIZARD

Lyrics by
E. Y. HARBURG

Music by
HAROLD ARLEN

We're Off to See the Wizard - 3 - 1
31909

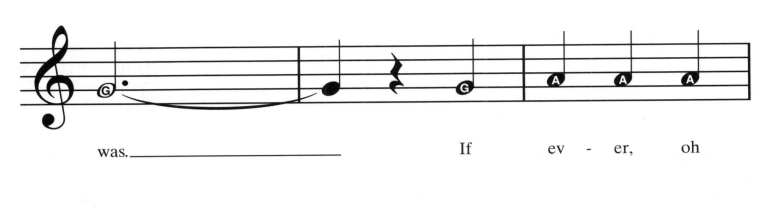

was._____ If ev - er, oh

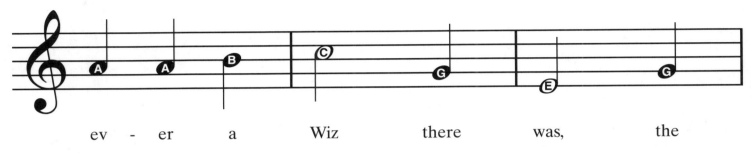

ev - er a Wiz there was, the

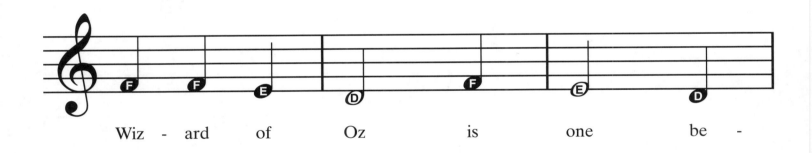

Wiz - ard of Oz is one be -

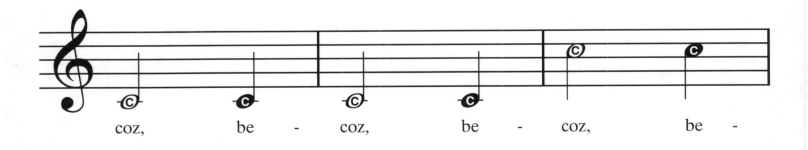

coz, be - coz, be - coz, be -

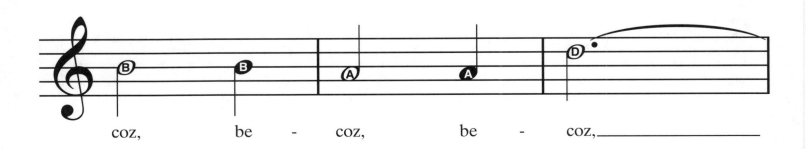

coz, be - coz, be - coz,_____

be -

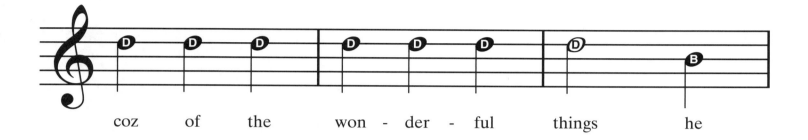

coz of the won - der - ful things he

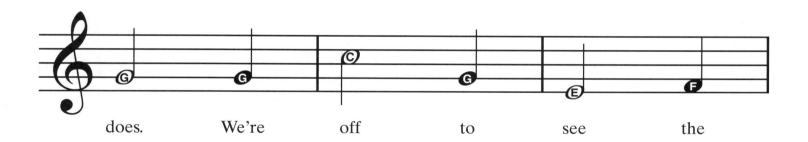

does. We're off to see the

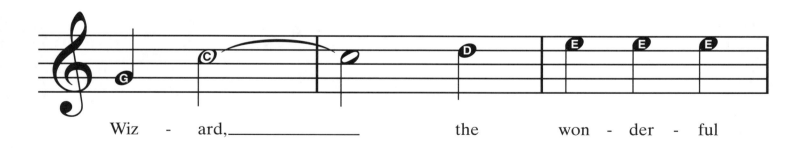

Wiz - ard,_____ the won - der - ful

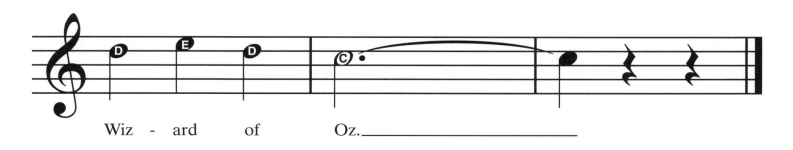

Wiz - ard of Oz._____

We're Off to See the Wizard - 3 - 3
31909

OVER THE RAINBOW

Lyrics by
E. Y. HARBURG

Music by
HAROLD ARLEN

Slowly with expression

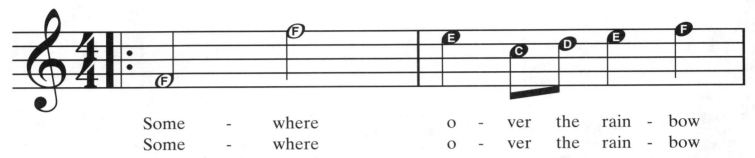

Some - where   o - ver the rain - bow
Some - where   o - ver the rain - bow

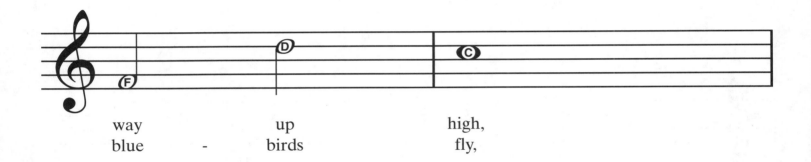

way   up   high,
blue - birds   fly,

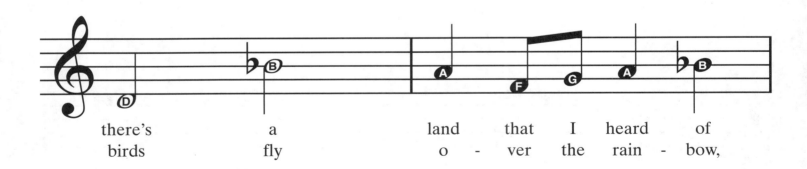

there's   a   land that I heard of
birds   fly   o - ver the rain - bow,

once in a lul - la - by.
why then, oh why can't I?